Life Goes On

Joe Tallarigo

Best wishes!!

Joe Tallary

Written and designed by Joe Tallarigo

Revised Edition

First published in 2017

Copyright © 2018 by Joe Tallarigo

ISBN-13:
978-1986032698

ISBN-10:
1986032698

To buy copies of Joe's books visit joesbook.webs.com

Life Goes On

The poems in this book reflect the years 2009 through 2015.

The first chapter is how I felt in life while dealing with my aunt's, uncle's and grandma's deaths in 2008, then having to deal with my mom's diagnosis of a terminal illness in 2009. I also had personal issues I had to face and deal with, which added more strife to my life. In the summer of 2009, I began watching a tv drama that resonated with me and helped me figure out some of my personal issues and help me cope with their deaths and my personal situation.

The second chapter is about my mom's passing in October of 2011 at the young age of 56. Then I write about growing up as a kid in Price Hill and my grade school days at Saint Lawrence during the 1990's. I also write about the different places my parents took my brother and I around Cincinnati.

I then move onto events like Major League Baseball opening day which is celebrated like a national holiday for Cincinnati Reds fans. I also write about Sean Casey and Joe Nuxhall, two of the nicest Reds players I had the pleasure of meeting through the years.

In 2013, I attended my ten-year high school reunion and reconnected with my classmates, then I focus on about turning thirty and hoping my thirties are just as good as they were in my twenties.

In 2014, the city of Cincinnati tore down my childhood home to build a new boys and girls club. Though my family moved from there in 1997, it was a part of me and I hoped one day we would move back in there, but that day never came.

In July of 2015, during the Major League Baseball All-Star Break, Cincinnati Mayor John Cranley, Reds owner Bob Castellini, Major League Baseball Hall of Famer Joe Morgan, and current Major League Baseball Commissioner Robert Manfred Jr officially opened the new boys and girls club. For me it was cool to have some baseball royalty standing where I learnt how to play baseball, and the fact that my first job in 2001 was with the Cincinnati Reds.

The third and final chapter is based on the four seasons of the calendar year.
My favorite season is Fall, when it gets cooler out and I can wear hoodies, build bonfires, go to high school football games, start decorating for Halloween, and then give thanks for what I have, and then start my Christmas shopping and going to Christmas parties and giving out gifts to the people I love and cherish.

Me in 1986

My First Day of Kindergarten
Saint Lawrence School 1990

In Memory of my Mom
Mary Ann

1955-2011

Acknowledgements:

Mom: Even though you're no longer here, your memory is kept alive through your blue vase collection and Christmas collection. And we still go to the places you visited. I miss you a lot.

My family: Thanks for all the support these past few years and the great times we shared. I know we been through some rough times these past few years, but we'll remain strong and closer than ever.

Lillian: Welcome to the family. Uncle Joe loves you.

Trinity Hill Daycare: Thank you for the support and helping our family when my mom was sick and after she passed away. It really means a lot to my family and me.

Class of 2003: Thanks to Kenny Combs, Ashley Burman, and Jenni Stadtmiller for throwing and hosting an awesome ten-year reunion. It was a great time catching up with everyone. I'm so proud of everyone and how far we've come since 2003. I can't wait for our fifteen-year reunion.

Collete Huff: Thanks for putting my first book *"The First Quarter"~ A Songwriters Dream* into the Country Music Hall of Fame bookstore. It means a lot to me and helped make my dreams come true.

Lee Family: Condolences to the loss of Arlene. Though I only met her a few times, I could see she was truly a wonderful woman.

To my readers: I hope you enjoy and take in these songs. I write from my experiences and make them relatable. This book is a journey of life and trying to get through the good and bad times. If I inspire even one person to follow their heart and chase their dreams, then I did my job.

Chapter 1

Bête Noire

2009-2011

The First Day we Met

The first day we met
our egos were flying high
we both wanted control
of the situation
we battled over jurisdiction
who would give in first
deep down I knew it wasn't going to be me
I'm a stubborn man set in my ways
but I always get the job done

You were conflicted with your loyalty
a woman who follows orders to a "T"
but we were losing time
trying to find a straight line
I asked whose team you would be on
I suggested you joined my team
until you made up your mind

That night was long
as we tried to find peace
we were two stubborn souls who wanted control
we didn't care who we injured
or stabbed in the back
as long as we made it out on top.

Paris Nights

Danger lurks around every corner
a dark shadow can kill with a single shot
but our laughter drowns out the danger we face
we gaze lovingly into each other's eyes
drinking red wine
wondering if we'll make it out alive
in these Paris nights

Being close to you
makes me feel secure
knowing our success depends
on both of us doing our jobs
I trust you'll follow your orders through
and everything will turn out alright
you may be new in town
but you're doing just fine
in these Paris nights

I wish we could climb the Eiffel Tower
to share a midnight kiss, as we look out over the city
but it's only wishing on my part
since we have a job to carry out
in these Paris nights

Capture or death can come at anytime
but right now we're under covers
sleeping safe and sound
I hope this mission ends soon
and we can get back home
to get out of these
Paris nights.

Two Year Plan

I held back my true feelings
I don't like getting too attached
since I get burned out too easily
I've had enough goodbyes and tears
these past few years to last me a lifetime

I was young and wanted to be on the run
I didn't want to be tied down
I wanted the freedom to fly out of town
on the whim
I should have been honest with you
but this isn't a book or a movie
this was real life, my life

I just stay around for two years
and I move on, even if I'm having fun
the rambling in my soul
is too strong for me to stay in one place for too long

I was young and wanted to be on the run
I didn't want to be tied down
I wanted the freedom to fly out of town
on the whim
I should have been honest with you
but this isn't a book or a movie
this was real life, my life

It's all about choices, I do what I need to do
but nothing will change how I feel about you
not even with my two-year plan
I hope one day you'll understand who I really am.

Shadow Man

He snuck in overnight
hid amongst the darkness
I know why he's here
he's going to pounce on my vulnerable heart
to shock the very core of my world
his intentions are clear
and I have every right to have fear

He's going to twist my arm
to get what he wants
and bring me harm
I'm scared to be here
wish he would disappear
but he stays in this room
preparing for his attack

I'm drowning in darkness
since he controls this situation
but I know my family and friends
won't let me down and will have my back
this shadow man
has to be taken out

White smoke begins to fill the room
shots ring out in the dark
I've been hit and I lay gasping for breath
he makes his escape
through the thick white smoke
but I know he'll be back again
to inflict even more pain on me.

Compadre Down

Proceed with caution
another compadre has been taken out of this fight
in another act of ignorance, another long night of sadness
it never gets easy to say goodbye

Here comes the rain again
washing away old friends, bringing in new troubles
this job is getting tougher
seems like it's all in vain
when one bad guy gets caught
another one steps up to the plate
and we're back on the chase
we're never safe or sound
when a compadre gets taken down

Rest in peace my friend
the ghosts of our past will haunt us to the end
I respect that you didn't reveal my secret
a secret that should have sent me away
but you're the one who took the bullet
and paid the price, but it's not right

Here comes the rain again
washing away old friends, bringing in new troubles
this job is getting tougher
seems like it's all in vain
when one bad guy gets caught
another one steps up to the plate
and we're back on the chase
we're never safe or sound
when a compadre gets taken down.

Smoke and Mirrors

I did things in my own way
trying to get you to believe my side of the story
though I wasn't upfront and honest
but I knew you would follow my orders to a "T"
and wouldn't let me down in my time of need

I put up smoke and mirrors, twisted the truth
covered my tracks
put people I loved undercover
brainwashed them into thinking
they were in the right
but something went astray
my plan blew up in my face and I got played
now there's repercussions for my actions

I feel like a fool for getting screwed over
I was so close putting my demons away
but someone else had to have a say
never trust those closet to you
you have everything to lose
when they expose the truth

I put up smoke and mirrors, twisted the truth
covered my tracks
put people I loved undercover
brainwashed them into thinking
they were in the right
but something went astray
my plan blew up in my face
and I got played
now there's repercussions for my actions.

Closing the Door to my Heart

I'm closing the door to my heart
everyone is tearing it apart
rumors spread through the rooms
people twist everything I say
they want to know everything
where I'm going, who I talk to
then they make up stuff that isn't true

Why can't they keep their mouths shut
they bring me down when I'm up
I don't understand the right they have
to stick their nose in my business
everything is fine on my part
but I'm closing the door to my heart

I'll tell them what they need to know
they don't need to know every detail
some of it is life's dreams, crazy schemes
but they all want to know
every move I make, everything I say

So I'm closing the door to my heart
leaving everyone in the dark
rumors spread through this town
when I'm not around
why can't they see
I'm just being me.

Nature of the Beast

Foxes steal and eat chickens
wolves travel in packs and howl at the moon
teenagers ask for money and car keys
toddlers don't follow instructions
politicians say one thing and do another
preachers preach forgiveness and the end of times

That's the nature of the beast
old habits are hard to break
you get what you see
to say the least
you shouldn't feel like a fool
if they pull the wool over your eyes
and screws you over
that's the nature of the beast

It's like trying to hit the big jackpot in Vegas
using every trick in the book to your advantage
but they always have eyes on you
better not slip up in your charade
though you shouldn't try to cheat in the first place
because the house always wins

That's the nature of the beast
old habits are hard to break
you get what you see
to say the least
you shouldn't feel like a fool
if they pull the wool over your eyes
and screws you over
that's the nature of the beast

So why do we try to do good
only to slip up again
we end up losing faith in ourselves
and hurt the ones we love
it's in our blood to want power and respect
even if we cross a line we can't come back from
that's the nature of the beast.

Frame-Up

You know I would never do wrong
I'd never break the honor code
I know it looks bad now
the evidence says I'm guilty
I could be going to prison
but you have to believe me
this is a frame-up

I've ticked people off
and let good woman down
some want revenge
yes, that must be it
because I would never cross the line
of good and evil
you have to believe me
this is a frame-up

I'm pacing back and forth
ready to pull out my hair
I'm not willing to face a judge and jury
who'll have no problem convicting me
on the evidence they have
someone please save me
this is a frame-up

Time is running out, I see the signs
I'm heading to prison
but I have faith a miracle will occur
that the ones who framed me will be found
and I'll be set free
from this frameup.

Bury Your Dead

We all must come to terms
that sometimes in life
we want revenge on those who hurt us
we stay up for weeks coming up with the perfect plan
to end the pain that eats us alive
we want to pull the trigger and watch them bleed

Bury your dead, hurt, and pain
it's all over now, does it feel good what you did
though it may have been justified
you just crossed a blurred line
and the cycle of revenge will come back around to you
bodies will keep piling up on the ground
until someone gives in and calls for a truce

Is your mental anguish really over
did you find the closure you were looking for
are you happy that you did it your way
putting your life and career in jeopardy
you may not survive the investigation to come
and might be prosecuted
but it's your life, I only have to this to say

Bury your dead, hurt, and pain
it's all over now
does it feel good what you did
though it may have been justified
you just crossed a blurred line
and the cycle of revenge will come back around to you
bodies will keep piling up on the ground
until someone gives in and calls for a truce.

Bourbon and Songs

I'm a tortured soul
who has lost too much in this world
I was too young to understand death
and the pain drove me to the edge
so I closed up shop and locked myself away
I began drinking and wrote songs about my pain

The bourbon burns, the songs heal
I wish you were still here
and I could end these tears
but finding closure keeps me going
and after all these years
the bourbon burns, the songs heal

I do my own thing
make my own rules
I don't allow anyone to come close to me
I don't want to get hurt anymore
twice was enough
three times would be too much

The bourbon burns, the songs heal
I wish you were still here
and I could end these tears
but finding closure keeps me going
and after all these years
the bourbon burns, the songs heal.

Playing with Fire

I'm at my wits end at how much more pain I can handle
my defenses are weakened
the thunder and rain won't leave me alone
and you keep pushing my buttons, not knowing

You're playing with fire
I'm the lighter, you're my gasoline
you're in my crosshairs and I'm ready to take you out
if you say or do one more thing to me
you won't see me coming
you'll be burned in an explosion of my anger
I'm tired of your childish ways and games
one day I'll finally be free from you

You may have won some battles
but I'll win the war
you can't keep a good man down
when he has everything to lose
so keep running your mouth
and bragging about your ego
one day you'll slip up and make a mistake
and I'll swoop in and take you out

You're playing with fire
I'm the lighter, you're my gasoline
you're in my crosshairs and I'm ready to take you out
if you say or do one more thing to me
you won't see me coming
you'll be burned in an explosion of my anger
I'm tired of your childish ways and games
one day I'll finally be free from you.

Get Out of Dodge

Get out of Dodge while you still can
blood will soon be spilt upon this land
let the women and children go first
so they won't see the worst
the men will stand their ground and fight

These outlaws have burnt down homes
robbed trains, put Sheriffs and their deputies in graves
now it's up to us
to put an end to their madness

Get out of Dodge while you still can
blood will soon be spilt upon this land
let the women and children go first
so they won't see the worst
the men will stand their ground and fight

The dogs are on guard, listening for any sound
the men are sleeping with their guns
ready to defend and put up a fight
they know the outlaws will run out of luck
once they cross the county line
they won't be terrorizing anyone after tonight

Get out of Dodge while you still can
blood will soon be spilt upon this land
let the women and children go first
so they won't see the worst
the men will stand their ground and fight.

Truth and Consequences

I feel like all eyes are on me
questioning my loyalty to my team
seems they believe I turned my back on them
it feels like a bad dream
a hall of illusions
I can't come to a single conclusion
and no one can help me
figure out what this is all about

Then a voice whispers
it's all about truth and consequences
who'll be the last one standing once the smoke clears
we've already lost so many in this game
isn't it time we find peace
and put the past to rest

But the memories play on
I can still feel the hurt and the pain
alibis are given, alibis are taken
some can be forgiven
but some burn in our memory forever
I can't forget the blowback
when they said you weren't coming home
why did you have to die

Then a voice whispers
it's all about truth and consequences
who'll be the last one standing once the smoke clears
we've already lost so many in this game
isn't it time we find peace
and put the past to rest.

Judgement Day

I made my bed and slept in it
didn't tie up loose ends, made mistakes along the way
I kept secrets and tried to be strong
but who was I kidding, I was weak
now my past is coming up in a whirlwind of dust
and it's coming down in whom I can trust

The nights were long, the days were short
I can still hear our laughter when we were undercover
how I long to be in your arms again
now here it comes down to my end

They came in like a thief in the night
slicing and dicing
until they figured out who they truly were looking for
I could hear their ringleader proclaim from his throne
that my time was up

I held onto my convictions from my past
I should have told you we didn't make a clean get away
now they are here for my judgement day, I hid to protect you
now I'm all alone to face my demons
I'm not leaving until I clean up my mess

They came in like a thief in the night
slicing and dicing
until they figured out who they truly were looking for
I could hear their ringleader proclaim from his throne
that my time was up

The time has come for my judgement day.

Cursed if you Do, Cursed if you Don't

Cursed if you do, cursed if you don't
it's like going against the current in a boat
no matter what you do, someone will complain
and accuse you of being wrong, even if you're right
the lines are getting blurred
but we continue on down the line
until some troublemaker comes along and unwinds the rope
and we're at the beginning again

We collect people's secrets and find their weaknesses
hoping one day to use them against them
but it only eats us alive
as we wait for the right time
to tell the world of their misdeeds
but we find they moved on
and they don't care who knows
so we try to bring them down in another way

Just trying to make a living is hard enough
but having a monkey on your back makes it even harder
we all have skeletons in our closets
had our moments of weakness
things we wished we would have done differently
but it is, what it is
and always will be
we're cursed if we do, cursed if we don't.

Swan Song

He was a man built by his own rules
could shoot a colt 45 by the age of nine
Western ways and cowboys influenced his life
said yes ma'am to the ladies and fought for their honor
but he was painted into a corner by his muses
and misunderstood for crossing the line
of law and order

He enjoyed his booze
hid guns and knives in his boots
could be counted on for helping out his friends
and tied up all their loose ends
then always walked away when the job was done
never wanted recognition or medals
just call on him and he'd fly in
but his time was closing in

He counted the way he could have done things
his rules made him king of the streets
no paperwork was ever filed
for putting the bad guys away
because he never took them alive
was he a hero or an outlaw
no one could say for sure
but he always got the job done
and this is his swan song

One rainy night, just like all the other rainy nights
he put up one last fight
protecting his friends from the enemies
but this time it cost him his life
when the blade went in, blood came out
he was one second too late
to pull the trigger
one second too late to save the day
his gun was always his ace

He counted the way he could have done things
his rules made him king of the streets
no paperwork was ever filed
for putting the bad guys away
because he never took them alive
was he a hero or an outlaw
no one could say for sure
but he always got the job done
and this is his swan song.

Reveille

My gut is telling me something is amiss
bad dreams and the shadow man haunt me
mocking me for being one step behind
I'm tired of him being free
he's got to pay for the harm he's caused
I'm not going to stand on the sidelines anymore
it's time to kick down his door
and find the S.O.B

There's no time to waste
we have to find out his name
so I can have it engraved on his tombstone
it's time to put an end to his mind games
it's been a little too quiet around here
it's time to end this fear
(Reveille)

Everyone be on high alert
he's killed once and may again
he'll spin his lies to justify his actions
let's get moving, leave no stone unturned
or we may get burned

There's no time to waste
we have to find out his name
so I can have it engraved on his tombstone
it's time to put an end to his mind games
it's been a little too quiet around here
it's time to end this fear
(Reveille.)

Twilight

Time is standing still
is this real or a bad dream
did he really just pull another trick
out of his sleeve
I thought we had him cornered
and ended his cat and mouse game
but I never saw this coming

Now twilight has set in
I let another friend down
I'm in shock, I can't move
it's a punch to my gut
now we have to say goodbye
since I let the twilight set in

I wish I could move the clock back
just before he got off his shot
but he won't be free too much longer
he just upped my anger
I won't be taking any prisoners
it's going to be him or me
but I have to allow myself to grieve

Now twilight has set in
I let another friend down
I'm in shock, I can't move
it's a punch to my gut
now we have to say goodbye
since I let the twilight set in

It's time to say goodbye
pay our last respects
we're going to miss your heart of gold
the smile on your face
nothing ever will be the same
since I let the twilight set in.

Chapter Two

I'm Still a Hometown Kid/ Road to Thirty

2011-2015

Weird!

Weird! That's all I can say
that's all I feel
I've lost loved ones before
but it's something more when it's your mom or dad
knowing they won't be around anymore
to give you advice or cook you a homemade meal

Strange! How I still pick up my phone
and dial your number
but instead of you answering
all I get is a dial tone
damn this emptiness again
why won't it end

Odd! How life turns out
at one point the pieces fit perfectly
now some have fallen out of place
some never to be replaced
no matter how much we try
to fill our hearts with hope and joy

Sad! The first thing I forgot was your voice
though I heard it everyday
if I had a choice I'd rather hear your voice
than to receive any heirlooms
better yet I wish you were still here
and live another fifty years

Though it's weird now
I know one day, we'll be together again
and everything will be right again.

Mom

I'll always remember our vacations
all our trips around town
Sunday and Tuesday night Bingo's
family and holiday get togethers
you always made sure everyone was there
and we all stayed in touch
you wanted the best for everyone
though life wasn't always fair

I'm sorry you never got the garden you wanted
I hope one day I can build one in your honor
and you can water it with your tears from Heaven
but I always smile when I see a butterfly
as I recall how you loved them
the Springs and Summers aren't the same anymore
without you, things aren't as fun

But I keep your memory alive
placing your mementos out in the open
I tear up in stores when I see snowmen or blue vases
that you would have added to your collection

I'm glad we got to see the ocean
though we never got to see a lighthouse
one day I'll go to one
and leave your photo behind
so you can look out over the ocean forever.

Sacred Place

Excuse me lady, while I have this moment alone
I don't expect you to understand what I'm doing here
I don't need you around for this moment of silence
as I wait for the ghost of yesteryear to appear
showing me what used to be
when I would come in early to hang out with my mom
this is a sacred place

Though she's gone
she made this her room
decorating it for every season
taking care of the babies like they were her own
a lot of good times took place in this room
no one can ever take that away
even if the rooms get rearranged
it's always going to be a sacred place

There's still an open wound many still feel
there was no closure, no way to deal
there may come a day we'll heal
just let me be so I can remember the memories
I'll get out of your way
as soon as it becomes clear
that I can move on
but even when I do
this room will always be a sacred place.

House on Top of the Hill

It may not overlook L.A. or the Pacific Ocean
it may not face snowcapped mountains
nor is it deep in the woods of Tennessee
where the black bears roam
it's not on Park Place
where money flows through the streets
but this house on top of the hill is where I call home

Every morning I watch the sunrise
rising over the Carew Tower
the cars coming in and out of downtown
and the Cincinnati Reds and Riverfest fireworks
from my balcony
I feel like a millionaire living in
this house on top of the hill

I watch the boats on the Ohio River
wishing I was on board
I love watching the storms blow through
and taking pictures of the rainbows
I've seen a lot since moving here
in this house on top of the hill

Every morning I watch the sunrise
rising over the Carew Tower
the cars coming in and out of downtown
and the Cincinnati Reds and Riverfest fireworks
from my balcony
I feel like a millionaire living in this house on top of the hill.

Ohio River View

I'm Still a Hometown Kid

I'm still a hometown kid
though I'd like to be living in Detroit or Nashville
putting down new roots, looking for new thrills
but the highways and backroads
always lead me back to Cincinnati

Who am I kidding, I love my city
LaRosa's pizza, Graters Ice Cream
The Big Red Machine, Kings Island, Skyline Chili
attending a little church on Sunday's where God still resides
there are days I'd like to make my escape
but at the end of the day
I'm still a hometown kid

My city is growing, the nightlife if glowing
from concerts, ballgames, music festivals
all the new businesses down at the Banks
and the beautiful gardens and playgrounds at Smale Park
though some of my family and friends have moved away
I feel like I belong here to my dying day

I'd like to visit the Black Hills of South Dakota
be a cowboy for a week out West
spend a weekend in Paris taking in the arts
backpack through the streets of Europe
learning about their cultures and myself along the way
but at the end of the day
I'm still a hometown kid.

Stormy Days

My mom always said when the leaves turn white
it's going to be a dark and stormy night
so when I saw the leaves turn inside out
I'd sit under the sycamore tree in our front yard
watching in awe, as Mother Nature unleashed its fury
bringing rain, hail, and high winds that caused trees to bend

Everyday I watched the Weather Channel
and one particular morning when I was in third grade
the weatherman said we were under a high risk
for severe storms
I became excited when the sky turned dark at noon
and as I ate my plate of chicken and noodles at lunch
in the cafeteria
a teacher who was outside for recess, came rushing in
said there's a tornado coming our way
so our teachers made us get under the tables
and we prayed The Hail Mary as the storm blew through

Some summers while swimming at Phillips Swim Club
gray clouds would gather overhead
the lifeguards would blow their whistles
as the claps of thunder echoed in the sky
we would rush out of the pool, get dried off
and tried to get home before the storm began

My favorite storms occurred at night
watching the vivid lightning light up the sky
feeling the house shake from the thunder
and hearing the hail bounce off the windows.

Ode to Grade School

In Kindergarten we went to Sunrock Farm
and I milked a goat
we got to bring in our favorite Christmas toy
for show and tell
in first grade I found out my cousin Andy was in my class
and at recess I caught bees with my bare hands

In second grade I learnt what it took to be
President of the United States
in third grade my dad chaperoned my class to the zoo
my fourth-grade teacher taught George Clooney
when he was in first grade
and I did a detailed report on Ohio

In fifth grade I got to sing Christmas Carols for my grandpa
at his nursing home
in Spring my class went to Camp Kern
where it rained all weekend
and we had to walk down five-hundred steps
to visit a school house built in the 1800's in the mud
and it was the final year my cousin Andy
went to school with me

In sixth grade I joined the school newspaper
"The Eagle Eye"
and the basketball team
in seventh grade I had my first crush on an eighth-grade girl
and began writing paranormal stories

In eighth grade I taught my classmates and teachers
how tornadoes form
and was excited that I would be attending Oak Hills
for high school
but sad that I had to say goodbye to my friends
whom I've known since Kindergarten
and in June I graduated
with a lifetime of great memories.

**(My Grandpa and me after the Christmas Concert
in Fifth Grade)**

Opening Day in Cincinnati

Call up the kid's school, our bosses
it's the only time we play hooky
we head down to Fountain Square
for the activities and giveaways
it's the perfect spot to watch
the annual Opening Day Findlay Market Parade
it's celebrated like an official holiday in Cincinnati

Everyone dresses up in red and white
a new season has begun
Bruce, Votto, Frazier, Arroyo, Cueto,
give us a reason to believe they can go all the way
and raise the first pennant flag at Great American Ballpark
they've come close these past few years

So let's cheer them on
I have the tickets in my hand
buy a program, hot dogs, peanuts, candy
forty-three thousand fans in the stands
waiting for the game to begin
there's a reason for hope
when the first pitch is thrown
come on down, cheer them on
for all eighty-one home games

Baseball fever has taken over
a whole new summer of hope and dreams
new legends are born and bred
not since 1990 have the Reds won a World Series
it's time they win it all.

The Mayor

He became The Mayor as soon as he walked
into Cinergy Field
at the start of the 1998 season
he was a fan favorite for many reasons
signing autographs, getting clutch hits
making the All-Star teams
he liked talking to the opposing players at first base
and got upset if they stole second base
if he wasn't done talking to them

Barry Larking was The Captain
Griffey Jr joined them as The Kid in 2000
but Sean Casey was The Mayor
a favorite, even amongst the other players
never stopped smiling for any reason
a Cincinnati Red for seven seasons
and still beloved to this day

In 2005 he was traded to his hometown of Pittsburgh
but the homecoming didn't last long
he was traded to the Detroit Tigers in 2006
hitting two home runs in the post season
then he was traded to Boston in 2008

Barry Larking was The Captain
Griffey Jr joined them as The Kid in 2000
but Sean Casey was The Mayor
a favorite, even amongst the other players
never stopped smiling for any reason
a Cincinnati Red for seven seasons
and still beloved to this day

Even though he's retired now
he still remains The Mayor
in 2011 the Reds fans elected him
to the Reds Hall of Fame
where his plaque now hangs
with Helms, Bench, Lynch, Cardenas, Davis, Sabo
and other players who have left their mark on this team.

Sean Casey and Me

Hamilton Joe

Did you ever imagine as a kid
you would play in the major leagues
at the young age of fifteen
what it must have been like
to pitch to Stan the Man
in your first game
history was made that night
for being the youngest player in the majors

After your pitching days were over
you moved to the radio booth
in 1974 Marty Brenneman joined you
both witnessing history for over forty years
starting with Hank Aaron's 714th homerun on Opening Day
Pete Rose becoming the hit king with hit #4192 in 1985
Tom Browning's perfect game in 1987
and the 1990 World Series sweep of the Oakland A's

You remained humbled and true to Cincinnati
always caring about the fans and the community
but in 2007 you rounded third and headed for home
still your legacy lives on
never to be forgotten
a regular Joe
born in Hamilton Ohio.

Joe Nuxhall and Me

Americana

I was four years old with my eyes covered
my sister said "you'll be fine, nothing bad will happen"
then the operator of The Serpent pulled the lever
and we began our ascent up the first big hill
my heart raced as we went up and up
I heard the screams as we went down, down, down
then side to side, up, up, up, down, down, down
I could hardly walk when I got off

It was our annual trip to Americana
a small-town amusement park in Monroe Ohio
in the midway you could play arcade games
and win prizes
swim in the pool
ride cable cars over Lesourdsville Lake
my parents, brother, sister and friends
hung out there from nine to nine
it was part of the great American experience known as
Americana

You could ride a big yellow slide in brown sacks
ride in bumper cars, flying helicopters
they had a log flume, paddle boats, the Electric Rainbow
I miss walking around the cowboy town
now that Americana closed down
I'll always cherish those summer memories

It was our annual trip to Americana
a small-town amusement park in Monroe Ohio
in the midway you could play arcade games
and win prizes swim in the pool
ride cable cars over Lesourdsville Lake
my parents, brother, sister and friends
hung out there from nine to nine
it was part of the great American experience known as
Americana.

Americana Photos

The Big Yellow Slide

Me and my Brother on a Turtle Statue

Riverfest

Blankets are placed on the Serpentine Wall by six A.M.
saving the perfect spot to view the fireworks
it's the last big party of summer
500,000 people on both sides of the Ohio River
spending twelve hours playing cards, tossing a football
eating and drinking with our friends
all for a thirty-five-minute firework show

Red, orange, blue, smiley face, heart, ring shaped fireworks
light up the September sky
everyone looks forward to the waterfall off the
Purple People Bridge
the party is loud, hot, and crowded
but it's always a good time
saying goodbye summer, see you next year

Classic Rock provides the perfect soundtrack
to pass the time until nine
then the city gets lit up
it's a party you don't want to miss
so come on down
join in on the fun

Red, orange, blue, smiley face, heart, ring shaped fireworks
light up the September sky
everyone looks forward to the waterfall off the
Purple People Bridge
the party is loud, hot, and crowded
but it's always a good time
saying goodbye summer, see you next year.

Stars and Pine Cones

I cherish the nights we'd sit on your front porch
watching the stars dance in the night sky
you called them balloons as we tried to count them all
but then you'd get distracted by the moon
and airplanes flying high

I cherish the days we'd spend in your front yard
collecting pine cones we found on the ground
we'd get fifteen to twenty at a time
then sort them smallest to biggest
and you cared for them as if they were your dolls

Oh, to be that young again, seeing the world anew
running through the grass barefoot
painting the world with different colors and hues
watching the sunsets with no regrets
never being too busy for family and friends

Stars and pine cones, painting, blowing bubbles
keeps me young as I do these things with you
I know one day as a teen you'll look back on these days
and you'll smile
that's why I do these things with you

Stars and pine cones.

The Big 3-0

I'm about to turn the big 3-0
though I still feel young at heart
wearing t-shirts and jeans
I'm still free to chase my dreams
there's no plan of me slowing down
I've been blessed with a good life
can't wait to start this next chapter
and see where the road leads me

I still want a wife and kids
the perfect job that'll allow us to travel
going to concerts is still high on my list
getting autographs from my heroes never gets old
I prefer cartoons to reality shows
I love eating pizza and ribs
turning the big 3-0 won't change that

Being in bars was never my thing
I prefer the outdoors
and listening to the Country Music classics
while driving on the back roads
taking photos of bucks and does
I'm still free to be me
as I turn the big 3-0.

Ten Years and Counting

Well it's been five years since our first high school reunion
and ten years since we've graduated
many have moved away, some made names for themselves
I'm proud their chasing their dreams
the same can be said for me
my first book is selling at
the Country Music Hall of Bookstore in Nashville Tennessee

It's good to see we're not too busy or too old to catch up
talking about the married life
while some are still looking for love
we're drinking wine, taking photos, making toasts
having a moment of silence for those who passed away
when we were eighteen
we didn't know where life would lead us
but for me these past ten years was a fun ride
and I wouldn't change a thing

Funny how time flies as we get older
yet reliving our glory days
seems to turn back the clock
if only just for tonight, as we celebrate our lives
reunions may seem old fashion to some
others choose not to come
but for me it's fun to catch up with friends

I hope the next ten years
will bring many more happy memories
the class of 2003 will always be special to me
it changed who I was
I want all the best for my friends
so now let's raise a glass and look around
we're just getting started in this town
here's to the next ten years and counting.

I Found Myself Missing You

I found myself missing you
so I called up our close friend
found out she was missing you too
isn't it funny how many times we wanted to visit
but always put if off
other times we'd drive by past your house
but didn't stop in
because we thought we'd be interrupting
or feel out of place
since we didn't call first
now we know it can be worse

How many goodbyes will it take to it finally sink in
that our loved ones can be taken out in a flash
yet we keep putting off what we love to do last
we tell our friends next time, I'm not up for it today
but then tomorrow never comes
we find ourselves asking why
why, oh why

I find myself going through old photos
crying to myself as I flip through the pages
feeling as if it was someone else's life
now I know time is a cruel joke
thought we had more time together
now we're laying flowers on your grave

I found myself missing you
so I called up our close friend
found out she was missing you too
isn't it funny how many times we wanted to visit
but always put if off
other times we'd drive by past your house
but didn't stop in
because we thought we'd be interrupting
or feel out of place
since we didn't call first
now we know it can be worse.

A Little Smile

A little smile can go a long way
a little hand will take you farther than a car
the world isn't so scary when someone believes in you
and guides you along
when you're afraid to take the first step
a little bit of faith and prayer is better than
wishing upon a star
take a look at where I've been
and where I am now
you can see your fingerprints all over my happiness

I wake up each morning to tackle the world
knowing I can make yours better
two hearts making it as one can be hard
but your faith in me calms my fears
though I shed tears cause the world is still dark
and people will do you wrong
I pray that one day people will change their ways
and you'll be safe

How does your childhood innocence still dwell in you
knowing what you've been through
a weaker person would have given up by now
or has my faith in you
like your faith in me
helped you see the pot of gold
at the end of the rainbow
you know

A little smile can go a long way
a little hand will take you farther than a car
the world isn't so scary when someone believes in you
and guides you along
when you're afraid to take the first step
a little bit of faith and prayer is better than
wishing upon a star
take a look at where I've been
and where I am now
you can see your fingerprints all over my happiness.

Maybe I've Been Wrong

Maybe I've been wrong all this time
running away from women and responsibilities
never learnt how to balance work and life
I love being single, though a part of me wants a bride
and have a child or two

When your father and mother
took you home for the first time
it opened my eyes
it was hard to leave after holding you
a baby in your arms is a gift
no one should take lightly

I want to give you cousins to play with
when you come and visit
it's time I take a look in the mirror
change my beliefs
stop letting my life pass me by
I need to be more confident when it comes to women
I'm ready to take the big leap
and settle down

Stay as young as you can
never let a moment pass you by
to make your parents proud
I hope you have a gypsy soul
and travel the world
set your dreams on the highest mountain
never settle for anything less
because you've been blessed

Maybe I've been wrong all this time
letting life pass me by
time I start thinking about my future
and find my better half
and leave my past behind.

My Childhood Home

Both sides of the family came over
for birthday parties
friends were always welcomed inside
we played video games, drew pictures to sell
played with our toys
made up our own adventures
played football in the living room
it was a house full of love and joy

I'd watch the storms move in from the West
on the large hill that was our front yard
my brother, friends and I would walk
to Braun's Deli for nickel and dime candy
went to Rally's for fries and shakes
we played tag, hide and seek in Radel's Funeral Home lot
those were the days of innocence and fun

We moved out in 1997
and when we drove past it
deep down I wished we still lived there
and hoped that one day we'd moved back in
but that day never came

The city tore it down in 2014
and during the Major League Baseball 2015 All Star break
Bob Cranley (Cincinnati's Mayor), Reds owner Bob Castellini
Reds and Major League Baseball Hall of Famer Joe Morgan
and Major League Baseball Commissioner Robert Manfred Jr
stood on the site of my childhood home
where I learnt how to play baseball
as they dedicated the Boys and Girls Club

I hope they know
family parties were held there
friends were always welcomed inside
we played video games, drew pictures to sell
played with our toys
made up our own adventures
I'd watch the storms move in from the West
on the large hill that was our front yard

It was a house full of great memories.

Me and my Brother on Dewey

Life Goes On

Sold my dad's vintage baseball cards
trying to make an extra dollar
didn't know they were worth so much
since I was only nine
when he found out what I did
he didn't scold me

He said life goes on
you did what you did
can't change it now
I sure had some great times
buying those cards with my dad
and him telling me about the players
you're just a kid, but one day you'll find
you have to let go
even if you didn't want to
and life goes on, life goes on

Few years later during my senior year
talking to my girlfriend at her locker
I gave her back the necklace she gave me freshmen year
I said I need a break, my space, I'm going through changes

She said I'll miss our walks, our talks
studying together for tests, I wish you all the best
sometimes we have to let go
maybe down the line
we'll run into each other again
and recall our good times
I have to remember life goes on

Time goes by, minutes turn to hours, hours into years
one minute your eighteen
next your thirty bringing a new life into this world
and you realize

Life goes on
the past is the past
you walk on grass, sand, and water
the storms make us stronger
though we wish the days were longer
and we could be in control
but one thing always remains the same
life goes on, life goes on.

Chapter 3

Seasons Come, Seasons Go/ Holiday Blues

Mrs. New Year

Going to start this year off right
my girlfriend of four years
has recently been dropping hints
she's ready to get hitched
I'm happy and content
but willing to take the next step
so when the clock strikes midnight
I'll be on my knee
with her engagement ring in my hand

She's going to be Mrs. New Year
Mrs. new last name come June
Mrs. new home later this summer
can't be more excited to see her
walking up the aisle with her father
in a little white church

Five minutes to midnight
she has no idea what's coming
I've managed to keep it a secret since October
when I went out and bought the ring
I've never been so nervous in my life
here I go, asking her to be my wife

She's going to be Mrs. New Year
Mrs. New Last Name come June
Mrs. New Home later this summer
can't be more excited to see her
walking up the aisle with her father in a little white church

Happy New Year!!! I love you Honey!!!

My Winter Rose

Call me a fool for believing in love at first sight
but there was something about her that felt right
she was laughing along with me at my stories
even though we just met, it felt like I knew her my whole life
she was nice to all her friends
talked highly about her family
I knew she was the girl for me

She's my winter rose
she brightens my world
when the days are long and dark
and the cold brings in the snow
blanketing the city in white
my love will always be hers
now that she's my winter rose

I count my lucky stars
that we happened to meet
and exchanged smiles
we gave it a whirl
knowing love is never easy
but when I first saw her
I knew my heart would belong to her

She's my winter rose
she brightens my world
when the days are long and dark
and the cold brings in the snow
blanketing the city in white
my love will always be hers
now that she's my winter rose.

I Hate February

I hate February
and seeing family and friend's names in the obituaries
doesn't death know it's a month for love
but all February brings is sadness
and angels to Heaven above

The music has stopped playing
the world mourns another loss
another life gone too soon
good ole Waylon, Buddy Holly
a boy name Frank
my Aunt Sue
don't know what to do
when February comes around

I hate February
and it's twenty-eight days of ice, cold, and snow
Spring can't come soon enough
to end my winter blues
and the mourning for those I lost

I hate February
and seeing family and friend's names in the obituaries
doesn't death know it's a month for love
but all February brings is sadness
and angels to Heaven above.

I'm a Heartbreaker

I'm a heartbreaker
take me or leave me
lay all your cards on the table
see if you get a pair of hearts
and win the jackpot of love
but if you receive any jokers
you'll end up a fool

I love them, lead them on
I give them my best smile
then turn it all around
down a country mile
and leave them crying in the rain

I'm a heartbreaker
it's hard to take in
because our love was real and felt so good
but the roulette wheel kept spinning
and the ball landed on red seven

I build up my walls
set them up for the fall
when I put on the dreamy music
serve them fine wine and in an hour
we're both single again

I'm a heartbreaker
it's hard to take in
because our love was real and felt so good
but the roulette wheel kept spinning
and the ball landed on red seven.

To the Land, Man

She has her pink fishing pole
sleeping bag all rolled up
her clothes piled up on her bed
she's running around telling her
brother, mother, father
let's go to the land man, come on let's go
I'm ready why aren't you
pack up the van
and get to the land, man

Being cooped up all winter
isn't good for an outdoors girl
she's ready to go fishing
and swimming in the lake
driving her princess jeep on the back roads
visiting the cows and chickens
she's ready to go
let's go to the land, man

You can see a million stars
living in a trailer in the woods
there's a fire pit to make smores
no chores to do
a private weekend getaway
there's fresh air, wildlife, no calls to be made
what are we waiting for

Pack up the van, man
let's go to the land, man
start up the van, man
let's get on the road
onto the road, man.

I Live for This

Live like you were dying
that's what they say to do
so every night when I go to bed
I look back on my day
and give God my praise

Every March I get out my glove
baseball and bat
the smell of cut grass, fresh air
the way I play the game
seeing the fans in the stands
and if I make an error or the winning play
I wear a smile on my face
you know I live for this

I live for the cheers
meeting new people
the changes of seasons
wet, warm, cold
I want someone to hold
I like the action, satisfaction
of making people smile

I like to play my guitar
jamming with my friends
singing about woman, country living
throwing mementos in the crowd
shaking hands, signing photos, and hats
you know I live for this

I live for the cheers
meeting new people
the changes of seasons
wet, warm, cold
I want someone to hold
I like the action, satisfaction
of making people smile.

Tornado

The sirens have stopped wailing
it quit hailing
the thunder has stopped shaking the ground
it's now safe to go up and look around
has our town been turned upside down
or were we spared

The sky turned dark, the winds began to pick up
rain and golf ball size hail began to fall
so I got my wife, my kids, my dogs
some photos off the wall
we huddled close together in the basement
as the sound of a train roared overhead
we prayed to God to protect us and our neighbors

The schools, main street stores
were the hardest hit
telephone lines are down
power will be out for days
except for minor injuries everyone is okay
now it's time to come together
and rebuild with our helping and caring hands
no tornado will chase us off our land.

Spring Broke

My high school Spring break buddies
called me out of the blue
said we're going to live out our glory days one last time
we're not getting any younger
and our senior year trip if you recall it stormed all week
now we found the perfect time
to reclaim the fun we missed out on
so are you in, this is it

I replied softly, you caught me at a bad time
my wife and I just bought our first house
we're adjusting to the married life
in fact, we just got back from our honeymoon
if this was two years ago I would have gone
but I'm Spring broke on money and fun
I hope you all have a good time

They said we never saw you settling down
you were one of the last to leave our hometown
not to mention you swore off girls
said they were a heartache ready to happen
but we're happy for you, are you sure you can't go
explain to her how close we are

I replied softly, you caught me at a bad time
my wife and I just bought our first house
we're adjusting to the married life
in fact, we just got back from our honeymoon
if this was two years ago, I would have gone
but I'm Spring broke on money and fun
I hope you all have a good time.

Mama's Pretty Eyes

Stood at my wife's side as she was giving birth
when she gave one last cry, one last push
the doctor exclaimed your daughter is here
he then handed her to me
I quickly saw that she had her mama's pretty eyes
she had her mama's pretty eyes

As the years went by
she turned those pretty eyes
into sad puppy eyes
I gave in a few times
then a thought crossed my mind
that she would use her pretty eyes
to wrap a man around her finger

That day came sooner than I expected
but I could see that they were in love
so I took him aside
warned him any tears falling
from those pretty eyes
better be tears of joy
because I don't want to spend my golden years in prison

Soon the news came they were expecting
and on the day of the birth
as my son-in-law held his baby girl
I heard that familiar glee
she has her mama's pretty eyes
she has her mama's pretty eyes.

Mama, I'm Coming Home Today

Mama, I'm coming home today
I don't want to be away any longer
I've missed your home cooked meals
the way you got into the characters
when you read me books as a kid
I long for the smell of fresh baked cookies in the oven
and the loving you give me, even when I don't make it easy

I dreamt of you putting up laundry
on a warm spring day
as I slept in a cold steel box car
you then looked over the gate towards the street
wondering if I ever was going to walk back in
and Lord it felt like a sin running away chasing dreams
when I'm only thirteen

Mama, I'm coming home today
I don't want to be away any longer
I've missed your home cooked meals
the way you got into the characters
when you read me books as a kid
I long for the smell of fresh baked cookies in the oven
and the loving you give me, even when I don't make it easy

Don't hide my pictures or be ashamed of what I've done
it made me realize I'm not yet a man
but I promise I'm going to give you a helping hand
and be a better son, I'm done being on the run
the only running I want to do, is run back into your arms
and get back to the good ole days
before I jumped on the trains.

Dad Are You Proud of Me

Dad are you proud of me
I'm following my dreams
I joined the high school football team
I have a car, I have a job
even though I stay out late
I get straight A's

Dad are you part of me
do I have your eyes, your name
do I laugh like you
do I have the touch to melt girl's hearts
like you melted moms
do I have the strength to fight
until the end like you did

Dad how far away are you
can I call, send a letter
are you feeling better
mom said you had to go away
and that I would see you again one day

Dad I need to know
I can't go on
without knowing who you were
so I pray tonight you answer me
are you proud of me, part of me.

Songs of Summer

I hear a song in kid's laughter
as they run around the playground
I see a masterpiece being painted
as the sun goes down

I hear a song in the night breeze
as it blows through the trees
I hear a symphony being played
by the crickets and the frogs

I hear a song as the ball sails
over the fence for a home run
I see love blooming on the beaches
as teen boys and girls flirt

I hear a song in the fireworks
as they light up the summer sky
I hear people talking about good times
with friends in their backyards

I see a perfect ending
to the last summer day
as the sun sets in the West
waiting until next year
to do it all over again.

Lonely War

He was smoking his cigarette outside his tent
a blank stare in his eyes
he blew the smoke into the darkness
I asked him what's wrong
he replied why do you care
you're just like me, fighting for a cause
that can't be won with guns or tanks
I have a wife back home
ready to give birth to our first child
he continued

Uncle Sam wanted me
but it hasn't been easy
being on this side of the world
but this is the price I paid
my grandpa and dad
fought for the red, white, and blue
so I followed them in their boots
but I wish there was peace beneath these stars
this is such a lonely war

I said I was a loner
going city to city
couldn't find one that suited me
then one day I saw a sign that read Army of One
I knew right then and there
this was my calling
I continued

Uncle Sam wanted me
but it hasn't been easy
being on this side of the world
but this is the price I paid
my grandpa and dad
fought for the red, white, and blue
so I followed them in their boots
but I wish there was peace beneath these stars
this is such a lonely war.

When Soldiers Fall

A son, a friend, a soldier, a husband
all those in one, what a man
to be so young and brave
to fight for our countrymen
some who still don't understand
what it takes to be free

He always wanted to be a soldier
playing war games as a kid
but war isn't a game
you don't get extra lives
he was tough and strong
putting his life on the line

Now it's time to bow our heads
and pay our respects
remember our good times with him
don't you dare disrespect his name
for standing up for the U.S.A
doing what he always wanted
since he was a young boy
he answered the call
but when soldiers fall
it touches us all

He married his high school sweetheart
found out he was going to have a daughter
but he never got to hold her
he made the ultimate sacrifice
he's a hero in my eyes

Now it's time to bow our heads
and pay our respects
remember our good times with him
don't you dare disrespect his name
for standing up for the U.S.A
doing what he always wanted
since he was a young boy
he answered the call
but when soldiers fall
it touches us all.

Seasons Come, Seasons Go

Amy brought down the stars to me
from that October sky
she gave my heart a chill of an early fall
and a new thrill to my life
we had had the time of our lives
under the Harvest moon light

Then one day she left town
and broke my heart in two
now when Fall comes around
and I feel the cold Canadian winds
and see the stars
and the Harvest moon shine
all I think about is her

Sarah loved to dance in the rain
and smelling roses in the spring
I spun her around on the tire swing
She brought a new joy to my life
we had the time of our lives
by the glow of the fireflies

Then one day she left town
and broke my heart in two
now when Spring comes around
and the rain begins to fall
and roses began to bloom
all I think about is her

Seasons come, seasons go
the world keeps on spinning
though my heart is breaking
there's a time for love
a time for mending
there's always a new beginning
to every ending
seasons come, seasons go.

Fall

Apple cider, leaves change colors
pumpkins are being carved and placed outside on porches
sun sets by six
colder weather moves in
goodbye beaches, swimming, and picnics
hello football, hot chocolate, and bonfires
it doesn't get much better than this

Fall carnivals, caramel apples
kid's rides, face painting
woman knit afghans and scarves
summer love is fading fast
as everyone heads home from vacations
the memories of a lost love
will keep you warm on these chilly nights

I feel most alive
when the calendar flips from September to October
feeling the crisp air in baseball stadiums
as the playoffs and World Series begin
it's a month of love and hate
hoping your team has what it takes to win it all

Jumping in leaves, decorating for Halloween
getting ready for Thanksgiving and relatives flying in
so much to do in so little time
but I love doing it year after year
there is no better season
do I need to give any more reasons
to why I love Fall so much.

Jenny in the Stands

Fire in our eyes, both seventeen
the full moon shines brightly
just you and me wanting to be free
feel the magic of the stars
dancing on our skin
love is taking us on a journey
Jenny in the stands

Your lips colored like roses
your eyes shine like diamonds
as we dance together
waiting for our song to be played
I'm not going to be swayed by lover's games
I'm going to take it nice and slow
so take my hand
Jenny in the stands

Out of a dream there you were
sitting in the stands
with your friends
I know you felt the same
when I first came up to you
asking if you were enjoying the game
and wanted to hang out
Jenny in the stands

Jenny in the stands
taking my hand for the first time
being young, chasing our dreams into the sun
Jenny in the stands
I'm glad to be your man.

Haunted Hayride

Are you ready for a night of fright
and be scared out of your mind
on this haunted hayride
with every twist and turn
a new horror appears

Werewolves roam the country side
a young girl stands on her grave
shadows are seen in abandoned houses
vampire bats fly amongst the tree tops
zombies rise up from the ground
I wonder what else is around

There are Satan worshippers
practicing rituals out here
I think the Devil himself may appear
demonic faces are seen in mirrors
hey do you feel hot and smell sulfur
we might want to get out of here

The horse seems to be sensing something
clouds cover the moon and it's getting late
do you think the headless horseman is around
we're deep in the woods with no way out
better hold on to your head
I hear the sound of hoof beats coming our way

I'm the driver of this haunted hayride
a ghost of the underworld
taking you to your new home of Hell and fright.

Halloween Town

The full moon shines bright
streets are covered in leaves
cobwebs hang on porches
spiders feast on flies
kids get spooked as they walk by
the haunted house at the end of the street

Witches brew spells with toads and lizards
evil clowns paint their faces and hide out in the woods
waiting to scare people
if they dare enter at night
vampire bats fly high in the sky

In Halloween Town it's 365 days of fright
spells are made and cast
spiders are welcome to hang out
teens sit amongst the graves
trying to conjure up the dead
hey is that a black cat up ahead
but it's nothing out of the ordinary
here in Halloween Town

Colonel Hayes is the guest of honor
though he died in battle during the Civil War
his spirit comes back just for the night
to give the new citizens of Halloween Town a fright
that they will never forget.

Five O' Clock Sunset

It's a five o' clock sunset
darker than the pits of Hell
I'm in a bitter mood can't you tell
snow is falling and the winds are howling
I'm longing for Summer nights
so we can grill out with friends, sit outside on the porch
watching the kids chase fireflies and placing them in jars
making their own natural nightlights

We're huddled near the fire, getting cabin fever
the kids are jumping on furniture
the dogs are yearning for their walks
but ice is covering the ground
heck if I'm falling on my behind like I did last week
this darkness at 4:45 isn't helping, I'm ready for bed
forget dinner and watching my nightly shows
might as well snow all winter long
because I'm staying inside and dreaming of warmer weather

The Christmas lights offer a little bit of joy
but they will come down by New Year's Day
we still have months of frigid weather
and feet of snow has yet to fall
darn this time change making it dark too early
I go to work in the dark and come home in the dark
making me want to finish my reports on Monday
and call in sick the rest of the week

It's a five o' clock sunset
the only good thing about it is, soon it'll be summer
and I'll be outside again with my friends.

Holiday Blues

One less chair, one less plate on the table
no sweet potato pie for dessert
no hugs and kisses for the grand children from grandma
it's the first holiday season without her here
there's not a lot of cheer
no Christmas carols are being played on the piano

It was always our Christmas tradition to put up the tree
after filling up on mashed potatoes, gravy, and turkey
the boxes are out being unpacked
but the garland and lights shine a little less
there's no need to fret, we'll decorate like always
but in one aspect it's not the same

No black Friday shopping at four A.M.
few less presents being bought and wrapped
no more homemade Christmas cookies
being baked with the grandkids
even the Christmas specials aren't cheering us up
it's like Scrooge and the Grinch moved in with us

Happy holidays to you in Heaven
spending your time with other family member
who have passed on
if you could can you leave a present under the tree
wrapped in gold and silver
so we know it's from you
to help us get over these holiday blues.

We Never Did Make It Back

A weekend getaway in Vermont
led us to a Strawberry festival
with ice cream, cakes, and pies
we tried them all and gave them all thumbs up
we went and picked some strawberries for us
it's a memory I'll always cherish
and swore we would attend again every year

But we never did make it back
all that remains from that day
is a picture of the two of us
eating a slice of strawberry pie
set against a blue sky
I'm glad we found the festival and attended
it was just what we needed
to make us a closer as a young couple
just wish we could have made it back again

We went to Metamora, a little town in Indiana
to do our Christmas shopping
the town was decorated in gold and silver
Christmas wreaths hung on the doors of the shops
a big tree stood in the center of town
decorated with ornaments and lit up by a thousand lights
the manger scene with baby Jesus
was such a beautiful sight
thought we found our new Christmas tradition

But we never did make it back
for one reason or another
all the handmade ornaments we bought
decorate our tree
a reminder of the fun we had
a Christmas outing with the family
but we never did make it back.

The Angel on top of the Tree is Weeping

The world stood still on the December day
shock on our faces as we watched the horror unfold
this Christmas will be filled with heavy hearts
because there's twenty young kids going to Heaven
Silent Night takes on a new meaning
and the angel on top of the tree is weeping

Another long battle lost in room 212
a young girl whose dream was to be an actress
and a young boy down the hall
who wanted to play football in the big leagues
the doctors did all they could
and the families now mourn alone
and the angel on top of the tree is weeping

I hope the angels have you in their arms
and you're no longer in pain
if I know my God
you're playing in the snow
and a special place at his table
please know you're not forgotten

Silent Night takes on a whole new meaning
the angel on top of the tree is weeping
and no words can heal the wounds.

Jack Frost Winds

Jack Frost winds are blowing in
can you feel the freeze on your skin
ol' Jack has been around
he knows the score
to chase everyone inside
when the weatherman talks about subzero wind chills

The bare trees are howling
blowing Christmas decorations down the street
snow is falling, creating whiteout conditions
ol' Jack is having a good time
creating a winter wonderland
for the Kids on Christmas break

Jack Frost winds are blowing in
pull out your sweatshirts and gloves
kids are building snowmen
dads are shoveling driveways
wishing they were watching tv
moms are snugged in bed
reading the latest number one book seller

Do you regret going out in the cold
Jack Frost is making himself known
hold onto your hat, it's getting brutal
listen to the winds howling through the bare trees
he knows the score
from December to March
he's the king
of the winter wonderland.

Winter Wonderland

I'm Dreaming of a Perfect Christmas

I'm dreaming of a perfect Christmas
where the whole family gets together
getting hugs and kisses, placing gifts beneath the tree
where snow is falling gently to the ground
and the Christmas town is all lit up
food is spread out on the table
I don't want much anymore
just a perfect Christmas will do

We're still pursuing the elusive perfect gift
and family has moved out of town
it's not like my younger days
when we celebrated on Christmas Eve and day
and both sides of the family came over
to exchange gifts
though I'm glad those memories we made
still resonate in the Christmas season

I'm dreaming of a perfect Christmas
where the whole family gets together
getting hugs and kisses, placing gifts beneath the tree
where snow is falling gently to the ground
and the Christmas town is all lit up
food is spread out on the table
I don't want much anymore
just a perfect Christmas will do

Going to the Cincinnati Zoo, Krohn Conservatory
and Fountain Square
were just some of the places
we would go to on those December days
now that we're older were passing those traditions
to our nieces, nephews, and cousins
and seeing their faces light up
makes it all worth it
though it's not the same without you
it's almost a perfect Christmas.

Our Christmas tree in my childhood home on Dewey

Merry Christmas Little One

What a beautiful sight to see
the Christmas lights reflecting in your eyes
snow is falling silently to the ground
the embers in the fireplace are dying down
hot chocolate will keep us warm
as we watch Christmas shows on tv
I lean over and whisper in your ear
Merry Christmas little one

Presents are wrapped beneath the tree
shepherds are keeping watch over their sheep
friends are stopping by wishing us a Merry Christmas
my little angel is sleeping by my side
golden hair in a red bow
she can't wait to play in the snow
I whisper in her year
Merry Christmas little one

Clock is reading ten
better get to sleep
let the sugar plum fairies dance in our heads
there's Christmas magic in the air
Santa will soon be here
but I already have the perfect gift
and it's free, I whisper in your ear
Merry Christmas little one

Sleep tight on this silent night
the angels are keeping watch over you
it's a Christmas now complete.

About the Author

Joe Tallarigo grew up in Price Hill a suburb of Cincinnati.
He spent his childhood hanging out with his older sister,
younger brother, and his friends who lived on Dewey
Avenue.
They would go to Radel's Funeral Home parking lot and play
baseball, football, tag, and hide and go seek. They would also
walk to Braun's Deli for candy, and to Rally's for fries,
hamburgers, and shakes.

He attended Saint Lawrence School from 1990 to 1999
where he played baseball and basketball. He was baptized,
received his first communion, and was Confirmed at Saint
Lawrence Church.

In 1997, his parents moved him and his brother to Delhi to
the house where their mother lived as a child.
After graduating from Saint Lawrence, he attended Oak Hills
from 1999 to 2003.
His first poem "Stay Around" was written on October 23,
2001, during his geometry class.
By the time he graduated he had written close to 40 poems.

His first book **"The First Quarter"~A Songwriters
Dream** was published in 2012 and bought by the Country
Music Hall of Fame and Bookstore.

His second book **"Country Outlaws and Dark Poetry"**
was published in 2016.

You can follow him at his website at joesbook.webs.com

More books from Joe Tallarigo

"Forever in my Heart~ Poems of my Youth"

"Country Outlaws and Dark Poetry"

You can follow Joe Tallarigo at Joesbook.webs.com for his latest signing appearances, order autographed copies of his books, and schedule appearances to speak to your class or group.
You can also find his books on Amazon.Com

Made in the USA
Lexington, KY
29 September 2018